THIS BOOK BELONGS TO

. . . .

THANK YOU FOR BEING OUR VALUED CUSTOMER. WE WOULD BE GRATEFUL

IF YOU SHARED THIS HAPPY EXPERIENCE ON AMAZON.

THIS HELPS US TO CONTINUE PROVIDING GREAT PRODUCTS, AND

HELPS POTENTIAL BUYERS TO MAKE CONFIDENT DECISIONS

COLOR TEST PAGE

Made in the USA
Monee, IL
29 November 2024

71617345R00046